D0842911

2/06

AnimalWays

Lions

AnimalWays

Lions

Rebecca Stefoff

Marshall Cavendish
Benchmark
New York

With thanks to Dr. Dan Wharton, director of the Central Park Wildlife Center, for his expert reading of this manuscript.

Marshall Cavendish Benchmark
99 White Plains Road
Tarrytown, NY 10591-9001
Website: www.marshallcavendish.us

Library of Congress Cataloging-in-Publication Data
Stefoff, Rebecca, 1951–
Lions / by Rebecca Stefoff.
p. cm. — (Animalways)
Includes bibliographical references and index.
ISBN 0-7614-1746-X
1. Lions—Juvenile literature. I. Title. II. Series.
QL737.C23S723   2004   599.757—dc22   2004011466

Photo Research by Candlepants Incorporated

Cover Photo: Peter Arnold/John Cancalosi

The photographs in this book are used by permission and through the courtesy of:
Peter Arnold, Inc.: S. J. Kraseman, 2; J. Pierre Sylvestre/BIOS, 29; Fred Bavendam, 44; John Cancalosi, 47; Roland Seitre, 55; Gerard Lacq, 59, 93, 96, 97; Denis-Huot/BIOS, 61, 74, 91; Kevin Schafer, 68; Y. Arthus-Bertrand, 70, 92; Gunter Ziesler, 77, 80; Martha Cooper, 85; *Corbis*: Paul A. Souders, 9; Phil Schermeister, 17; Roger Wood, 18; Bettmann, 20; Hulton-Deutsch Collection, 22; Jeffrey L. Rotman, 24; Tom Brakefield, 33, 40, 41, 43; Renee Lynn, 49; Yann Arthus-Bertrand, 63; Brian A. Vikander, 83; Keren Su, 86; Joe McDonald, 87, back cover; Mary Ann McDonald, 90; Craig Lovell, 99; AFP, 102; *Art Resource, NY*: Erich Lessing, 13; Reunion De Musees Nationaux, 14–15; *Kobal Collection*: Columbia, 26; *Minden*: Mitsuaki Iwago, 65; Michael & Patricia Fogden, 76.

Printed in China

1 3 5 6 4 2

Contents

Animal Kingdom

CNIDARIANS

coral

ARTHROPODS
(animals with jointed limbs and external skeleton)

MOLLUSKS

squid

CRUSTACEANS

crab

ARACHNIDS

spider

INSECTS

grasshopper

MYRIAPODS

centipede

CARNIVORES

LION

SEA MAMMALS

whale

PRIMATES

orangutan

HERBIVORES
(5 orders)

elephant

PHYLA

ANNELIDS

earthworm

CHORDATES
(animals with
a dorsal
nerve chord)

ECHINODERMS

starfish

SUB PHYLA

VERTEBRATES
(animals with a
backbone)

CLASSES

FISH

fish

BIRDS

gull

MAMMALS

AMPHIBIANS

frog

REPTILES

snake

ORDERS

RODENTS

squirrel

INSECTIVORES

mole

MARSUPIALS

koala

SMALL MAMMALS
(several orders)

bat

King and Queen of Beasts

1

The night breeze rustles across Savuti, a region of grassland and scattered forest near the Okavango Delta in the southern African country of Botswana. Animals are spread across the plain in a large, straggling group. Some are lying on the ground with their legs curled under them. Others move about slowly, grazing. Mothers nurse their young. The herd includes zebras, the small brown antelope called impalas, and the larger antelope called gnus or wildebeests.

A wildebeest snorts in alarm, and just then half a dozen large, tawny cats bound out of the darkness. The peace of the night is shattered. The herd leaps into panic-stricken motion. The impalas and zebras are first to run. The wildebeests are a little slower, perhaps because many of them were lying down. They lag behind—and the lions are among them, striking at anything within reach. The herd thunders away, but one wildebeest calf, no more than two days old, slips and falls. At once the calf

A LIONESS (LEFT) AND LION ON THE SAVANNA OF KENYA'S MASAI MARA NATIONAL RESERVE, ONE OF THE PARKS THAT AFRICAN NATIONS HAVE SET ASIDE FOR WILDLIFE.

scrambles to its feet and races to join the fleeing herd, but a lioness saw it fall and is charging toward it. The calf turns sharply to the left. Trying to follow, the lioness loses her footing in a patch of grass that is wet with dew. She falls behind for a second, and the calf turns back toward the galloping herd. To reach the safety of the herd, though, the calf must run past the lioness, who has regained her footing. She leaps onto the calf, and her weight drags it down. With one bite through its neck, she ends its short life and provides a meal for her family.

The death of that wildebeest calf on a December night in 1970 was one of almost fifteen hundred lion kills witnessed by two wildlife photographers named Dereck and Beverly Joubert. The Jouberts spent many years and thousands of hours watching, filming, and photographing the lions of Savuti. They were very aware that the lions around them were ferocious, determined predators and carnivores. Yet they also came to understand other things about lions: their family structure, their relations with other creatures, the rhythms of their days and nights. The Jouberts became so familiar with the cats that Dereck Joubert wrote, "For us there was nothing more comfortable than stretching out for a light sleep in the back of our vehicle with the soft, deep breathing of lions all around us, punctuated by the occasional snore or sound of grass rustling as one of them turned over."

People have always been fascinated by lions. For centuries the great golden cats have enriched folklore, art, and culture as images of power and nobility. Today, scientists try to understand lions—and all creatures—for what they are in the natural world, not as symbols of human qualities. The Jouberts are part of a group of researchers who have ventured into the lions' world to discover how these much-feared, much-admired animals live. Modern research is providing a new understanding of lions.

Their social structure and habits are more varied than people used to think, and their complex interactions with their environments are just beginning to be understood.

History, Legend, and Art

When the eighteenth-century British author Samuel Johnson wrote the first dictionary of the English language, he defined *lion* as "the fiercest and most magnanimous of the four footed beasts." That 1755 definition sums up the two qualities that people have most often claimed to see in lions. Lions are fierce indeed—strong, ferocious fighters and hunters who kill to eat and to defend their territories. But Johnson also called them magnanimous, which means "noble and generous." Since ancient times people have associated lions with strength and domination and also with noble, royal, even godlike dignity. These qualities earned the lion the nickname "king of beasts." The lioness, or female lion, is also admired. The ancient Egyptians even worshipped her as a goddess.

Before human cultures began writing down their histories and their legends, they celebrated lions in their art. On the walls of caves in France and Spain, prehistoric people painted magnificent, remarkably accurate images of the animals they saw, hunted, and perhaps worshipped. Lions prowl and pounce in these paintings, which are between thirty thousand and twelve thousand years old. Early inhabitants of North Africa also carved and painted images on rock walls. These ancient artworks show lions intermingled with the other animals—giraffes, antelope, and elephants—that roamed the Sahara ten thousand years ago, when the region was a moist grassland instead of the desert it is today.

Some of the earliest writings of ancient civilizations mention lions. Records from the time of the Egyptian pharaoh Amen-hotep III, who ruled from 1417 to 1379 B.C.E., say that during the first ten years of his reign, he killed 102 lions. That claim may or may not be true. Historians know that many ancient kings and warriors boasted of killing lions to emphasize their own might. In the same way, one of the legendary exploits of the mythical Greek hero Hercules was slaying an especially ferocious beast called the Nemean lion.

The Bible mentions lions as part of the wildlife of the Near East. Lions were numerous in Assyria (now part of Iraq) during the seventh century B.C.E. Carved into a stone wall from that time is an account of the predators' dire effects on the local population, as well as a hunter's boast: "The hills echo with the thunder of their roars. . . . The herdsmen and their masters are in distress. Women and children mourn. . . . On my hunt I have entered the lions' hiding places. I have destroyed their lairs."

Ancient Greeks wrote about lions living in Greece and nearby eastern European lands. The historian Herodotus says that when the Persian emperor Xerxes invaded Greece in 480 B.C.E., lions ate several of the Persians' baggage camels. The ancient Romans knew of lions, too. During the first century C.E. the Roman emperor Nero forced captive Christians to fight lions—the Christians lost. Lions were occasional performers in the hunts and combats that Rome's rulers staged until the sixth century in the giant arena known as the Colosseum.

Lions hold a powerful place in the myths, legends, and symbols of many cultures. The ancient Sumerians, Assyrians, and Babylonians, who lived in the semidesert land that is now Iraq, worshipped a god of rain, storms, and fertility who took the form of an eagle with the head of a lion. The sound of thunder was thought to be his roar. Sekhmet, a goddess with a woman's body and the head of a lioness, was worshipped by the ancient

THE LEGENDARY GREEK HERO HERCULES WAS SAID TO HAVE PERFORMED TWELVE DIFFICULT LABORS, OR TASKS, THAT BECAME POPULAR SUBJECTS FOR ILLUSTRATION IN GREEK ART. THE FIRST LABOR WAS KILLING THE NEMEAN LION, WHICH HAD BEEN PREYING UPON LIVESTOCK. HERCULES WAS UNCLOTHED BEFORE HE KILLED THE LION, BUT AFTERWARD, HE WORE ITS SKIN.

Egyptians, who associated her with war, vengeance, disease, and healing. In the Hindu religion of India, the god Vishnu appears in lion form as Narasingha.

In Hindu religion the god Vishnu, called the Preserver, takes ten different forms to save the human race. One form is that of the lion-god, Narasingha. The god's multiple arms are symbols of his divine powers and qualities.

Even in parts of the world where there are no lions, people have given them an honored place in their cultures. China has never had a native lion population, but more than two thousand years ago, princes and kings in Iran and other parts of western Asia began sending lions as gifts to the Chinese emperors. The lion entered Chinese mythology in the story of a fierce monster that ravaged the countryside, killing people and livestock. After the fox and the tiger failed to defeat the monster, the people of China asked the lion for help, and with one shake of its mane the lion chased the monster away. The lion was rewarded with the honor of guarding the gates to the emperor's palace, and the people learned to disguise themselves as lions to drive away the monster whenever it reappeared. The traditional Chinese lion dance, performed by two dancers in a costume, is based on this tale and is still performed in Chinese communities around the world.

Many imaginary creatures owe part of their anatomy to the lion. The sphinx, for example, has a lion's body and a human head. The griffin has a lion's body, hindlegs, and tail attached to the legs, wings, and head of an eagle. The chimera, a fire-breathing monster of Greek myth, has a lion's head on a goat's body with a dragon's tail, while the manticore, which appears in medieval European tales and illustrations, has a lion's body with a scorpion's tail and either a human or a leonine head. In all of these mythic appearances, the lion is a symbol of strength and power. The lion is also associated with royalty. Medieval writers who believed that the animal world mirrored human society considered the lion to be the supreme ruler of the natural world. Many royal and noble families linked themselves with this regal image by including the lions in their seal, coat of arms, or other symbols. The lion's power to suggest bravery, strength, and victory remains strong today. Hundreds, perhaps thousands, of sports

Costumed dancers in San Francisco's Chinatown, one of the oldest Chinese-American communities in North America, celebrate the Chinese New Year with a traditional lion dance.

THE SPHINX—A CREATURE WITH A LION'S BODY AND A HUMAN HEAD—GAZES OVER ITS MASSIVE PAWS AT THE DESERT SANDS NEAR GIZA, EGYPT. THE ANCIENT EGYPTIANS CREATED THE HUGE STATUE AROUND 2500 B.C.E. ITS HEAD IS THOUGHT TO BE A ROYAL PORTRAIT. ARTISTS PORTRAYED MANY EYGPTIAN RULERS AS SPHINXES, GIVING THEM THE SYMBOLIC STRENGTH AND PROTECTIVENESS OF LIONS.

teams around the world are named for these mighty animals.

Artists have used lions to represent many things. Sometimes the lion stands for the untamed power of the natural world. At other times it symbolizes the wisdom and protectiveness of a just ruler. As emblems of strength and security, lions appear in architecture all over the world, from the twin statues on the steps of the main branch of New York City's public library to the twelve marble lions that support a fountain in the Lion Court of the Alhambra Palace in Granada, Spain, and from the paired male and female lions that guard the gates of the Lama Temple in Beijing, China, to the massive bronze beast that is part of the Independence Monument in Mexico City.

From ancient times to the present, literature offers memorable lions. In the second century C.E. the Roman Aulus Gellius wrote of an escaped slave named Androcles who removed a thorn from a lion's paw and was later spared by the grateful beast when they met in the arena. In more recent years, a lion named Aslan appeared as a symbol for Christ in C. S. Lewis's widely read Narnia books for young people. The image of the brave lion was comically reversed in the figure of the Cowardly Lion in the book and movie *The Wizard of Oz*. The popular animated movie and Broadway musical *The Lion King* tells the story of a young lion who overcomes obstacles and finds allies on his quest to take his rightful place as ruler.

Africans have lived in close contact with lions for thousands of years. They have hunted lions, been preyed on by them, and struggled to protect their livestock from them. Among some African peoples, it is traditional for kings and chieftains to wear a cloak or sit on a rug made of a lion's skin. This use symbolically suggests that the wearer is powerful enough to kill the lion and take its strength for himself. Lions sometimes appear in African folklore as symbols of fierceness and anger, as in the Congolese

ACTOR BERT LAHR PLAYED THE COWARDLY LION IN THE 1939 MOVIE *THE WIZARD OF OZ*. HIS CHARACTER'S GENTLE TIMIDITY WAS A COMICAL SWITCH ON THE USUAL IMAGE OF THE LION AS BOTH FIERCE AND BRAVE.

proverb that says, "What is said over a dead lion's body could not be said while he was alive." At other times, however, the lion of African legend is a creature of brute strength who is rather dim-witted. He can be overcome or outwitted by smaller, weaker creatures who happen to be cleverer, as stated in the Ethiopian proverb: "When the webs of spiders join, they can trap a lion." In many folktales from South Africa, for example, the lion is king and ruler of all animals, but he is repeatedly tricked out of his food by the small, quick-witted jackal (a relative of the dog).

Varying Views

As Europeans began exploring and colonizing lion country in Africa and Asia, the lion became more than a distant symbol of majesty for them. It became a threat, a nuisance, and a hunting trophy. Writes Eric S. Grace in *The Nature of Lions: Social Cats of the Savannas* (2001), "The dominant Western view of lions from the mid-1800s to the mid-1900s was the view along the barrel of a rifle."

The British and other Europeans aggressively hunted lions in Africa and Asia for several reasons. One reason was sport. European hunters took pride in killing big game, and lions were among the biggest of their prizes. Cattle-herding African peoples, such as the Masai of East Africa, had always hunted lions—such a hunt was a test of manhood in some cultures. European rifles were far deadlier than African spears, however, and sportsmen could kill dozens of lions in a single hunt. Adventurers such as Theodore Roosevelt, a former president of the United States, flocked to Africa to take part in hunting expeditions called safaris. Roosevelt described his safaris in *African Game Trails* (1910), one of many African-adventure

A HUNTING PARTY IN EAST AFRICA AROUND 1895. LIONS WERE PRIZED TROPHIES FOR
EUROPEAN AND AMERICAN HUNTERS, WHO OFTEN DECORATED THE WALLS OF THEIR
HOMES WITH THE ANIMALS' HEADS OR SKINS. HIGH-POWERED HUNTING RIFLES LIKE
THOSE HELD BY SOME OF THIS HUNTER'S AFRICAN ATTENDANTS WERE THE KEY TO
THE FOREIGNERS' SUCCESS AT KILLING LIONS.

books that were wildly popular with American and European readers.

Another reason for hunting lions is that the great cats came to be viewed as dangerous pests that killed livestock and occasionally people. Lions were obstacles that had to be cleared away so that civilization could take root and spread. More than anything else, reports of "man-eating" lions brought this attitude to the surface. In 1898, reports of such lions came out of the Tsavo River region in East Africa, where the British were building a railway in what was then their Kenya colony. In a period of less than a year, more than 140 workers had been killed and eaten by a pair of lions. A hunter named Colonel J. H. Patterson shot both lions and then wrote *The Man-Eaters of Tsavo*, which painted a grisly picture of the workers' dreadful fates. More recently, the American writer Philip Caputo examined the incident in *The Ghosts of Tsavo* (2002).

A lion will not typically hunt and feed on humans, although it may do so if it is sick and unable to catch faster, more difficult prey. Two things probably contributed to the Tsavo attacks. One was an epidemic of rinderpest, a disease that wiped out millions of game animals such as zebras and antelope in the 1890s. With their usual prey grown scarce, the lions may have been tempted by the unprotected railway workers. In addition, burial practices at the labor camps were slipshod. If the bodies of dead workers had been buried in shallow graves and were easy to dig up, the lions could have gotten used to scavenging these easy pickings. Once they became accustomed to eating humans, they turned to live prey. Wildlife biologists believe that similar pressures and conditions have probably influenced most man-eaters.

Fear of lions as possible man-eaters drew audiences to public exhibitions of lions in the nineteenth and early twentieth centuries.

THE LION TRAINER FOR THE GREAT ROYAL CIRCUS IN BOMBAY, INDIA, FOLLOWS AN
OLD TRADITION. PREDATORS SUCH AS LIONS AND TIGERS HAVE BEEN PART OF CIRCUSES
AND OTHER ENTERTAINMENTS FOR MANY YEARS. WHEN TRAINERS GET CLOSE TO THE
GREAT CATS, AUDIENCES THRILL TO THEIR POTENTIAL DANGER.

In circuses and wild-animal shows, fearless lion tamers placed
themselves in harm's way by entering a cage with one or more
lions, often brandishing whips and chairs to keep the fierce
beasts in line. An American trainer named Isaac Van Amburgh

raised the stakes in the mid-nineteenth century by placing his head between the open jaws of one of his lions, an act that caused audiences to swoon with terror and amazement.

Concerns about wildlife and wilderness preservation gave rise to a new, more environmentally aware view of lions after the mid-twentieth century. Many nations took steps to limit the hunting of lions. Some established wildlife parks and game preserves as protected habitats for lions and other animals. More and more often, safaris were for people carrying cameras, not guns. At the same time, a wave of new studies shed light on the life of the lion.

One of the first and best-known books about lions from this period is *Born Free*, published in 1960 by Joy Adamson, an artist and the wife of a senior wildlife official in Kenya. *Born Free* was not a piece of scientific research—it was the personal story of the Adamsons' relationship with a lioness named Elsa. The Adamsons raised Elsa from cubhood and returned her successfully to life in the wild. Their poignant account of how they helped her reclaim her wild heritage became a best-seller in many nations and was made into a popular movie. *Born Free* opened readers' eyes to the marvels of all of Africa's wildlife— not just lions—and to the dangers it faced from illegal hunting and uncontrolled development. It also changed the way people thought about lions. George Schaller, a wildlife biologist, wrote, "The Adamsons gave us . . . a new image of the lion, an immensely appealing one of a playful, devoted, kindly, and even vulnerable creature; they gave us truths about the species that cannot be found in a biologist's notebook, hunter's tale, or tourist's account."

Schaller also provided truths about lions in his award-winning book *The Serengeti Lion* (1972). Based on three years spent observing East African lions, *The Serengeti Lion* is still

considered one of the most important books ever written about lions. It was one of the first full-length studies of the big cats' social organization, family life, and hunting methods. Together with many other research papers, books, photographs, and documentary films, it has enriched the view of the king and queen of beasts and of their kingdom.

THE 1966 MOVIE *BORN FREE*, WHICH STARRED BILL TRAVERS (SHOWN HERE) AND VIRGINIA MCKENNA AS GEORGE AND JOY ADAMSON, BROUGHT JOY ADAMSON'S STORY OF ELSA THE LIONESS TO AUDIENCES AROUND THE WORLD. LIKE THE BOOK, IT HELPED AWAKEN INTEREST IN AFRICA'S WILDLIFE AND THE CHALLENGE OF PROTECTING IT.

2 Origins and Varieties

Since cats first appeared about forty million years ago, hundreds of large and small cat species have evolved in various parts of the world. Most of them are long extinct. Thirty-seven cat species exist today, and biologists think that the lion—*Panthera leo*, in scientific terms—is one of the most recently evolved species, being a mere million years old or less.

Leonine Ancestors

All cats, past and present, belong to the large family of animals known as Felidae, or felids. Just as modern lions are descended from ancient felids, felids themselves descended from earlier ancestors that were not cats. Scientists have examined fossil bones, the DNA of modern cats, and felid behavior to trace the ancestry of felids.

AMONG THE EXTINCT LARGE FELIDS WERE VARIOUS SPECIES OF SABER-TOOTHED CATS. THEIR NAME COMES FROM THE LARGE, SWORDLIKE FANGS IN THE UPPER JAW. MODERN LIONS ARE NOT DESCENDED FROM THE SABER-TOOTHED CATS, BUT THEIR FANGS SERVE MUCH THE SAME PURPOSE AS THOSE OF THE ANCIENT BEASTS: TO STAB AND HOLD THEIR PREY.

Paleontologists, scientists who study the fossils and other remains of ancient life-forms, believe that cats and all other members of the order Carnivora (meat eaters) are descended from an early group of meat-eating mammals called miacids. Miacids were small, weasel-like carnivores that skulked in the underbrush and probably fed mostly on insects and worms. But the miacids had predatory potential—they are the oldest known animals to have carnassial teeth, the strong, bladelike teeth in the sides of the upper and lower jaws that all modern carnivores use for tearing the flesh of their prey. The presence of these teeth has led paleontologists to think miacids may have preyed on each other and other small mammals, as well as on insects and worms. The miacids eventually evolved into many different kinds of carnivorous predators in two broad groups.

The arctoids, whose name comes from the Latin words for "bearlike," formed one group (some scientists call this group the canoids, or doglike animals). Among the arctoids were the ancestors of modern bears, wolves, foxes, weasels, and raccoons, as well as many animals now extinct. The arctoids had carnassial teeth, but, like the ancestral miacids, they also had molars, flat-topped teeth for crushing and grinding vegetation. Having both kinds of teeth allowed the arctoids to eat a varied diet. Their descendants have retained this ancient tooth pattern—although they are carnivores, modern bears, raccoons, and even wolves can and do eat vegetable foods on occasion.

The other main group that evolved from the miacids were the aeluroids (catlike animals that some scientists call feloids). By about forty million years ago, aeluroids had evolved into several families. One family, Hyaenidae, contained the ancestors of today's hyenas. Another family, Nimravidae, contained many catlike animals. A third family, Felidae, contained the ancestors of modern cat species.

Over millions of years, the Nimravidae and Felidae families produced hundreds of species. Some of these creatures were similar to modern cats, while others were quite different. Scientists refer to the nimravids (members of the Nimravidae family), as paleofelids, which means "ancient cats." All members of this family had become extinct by two million years ago, leaving fossils but no living descendants. Felids are members of the Felidae family. Scientists sometimes call felids true cats or neofelids, which means "new cats." Although the Felidae family is as ancient as the Nimravidae family, felids have not died out the way the nimravids have. All living cat species are Felidae, as are many that have become extinct.

Both Nimravidae (paleofelids) and Felidae (neofelids), included saber-toothed cats, all of which are now extinct. These large carnivores had long, curved teeth hanging down from the upper jaw, which looked like the curved swords known as sabers. Fossil hunters in the nineteenth century, impressed with the massive skull and fearsome teeth of these ancient predators, sometimes called them saber-toothed tigers, although they were not tigers. Some of them were not even cats—at least two families besides the paleofelids and neofelids included large predators with saberlike teeth. The best-known saber-toothed predator, however, was a neofelid. It was a large cat called *Smilodon fatalis*, which appeared around two million years ago and remained in existence until about 10,000 years ago. *Smilodon fatalis* roamed across North America and left fossils in many places. The greatest concentration of them has been found at the La Brea Tar Pits in Los Angeles, California. At this site, sticky pools of naturally occurring tar trapped and preserved the remains of animals that ventured into them, including at least two thousand specimens of *Smilodon*.

Lions are not descended from *Smilodon* or from any of

the other ancient saber-toothed cats. Instead, scientists think that lions and all other living cat species descended from a single neofelid species. They have not yet identified it, but they believe that it lived between ten and twelve million years ago. This ancestral cat evolved into various lines of descent. Some became extinct, while others led to the cats of the modern world.

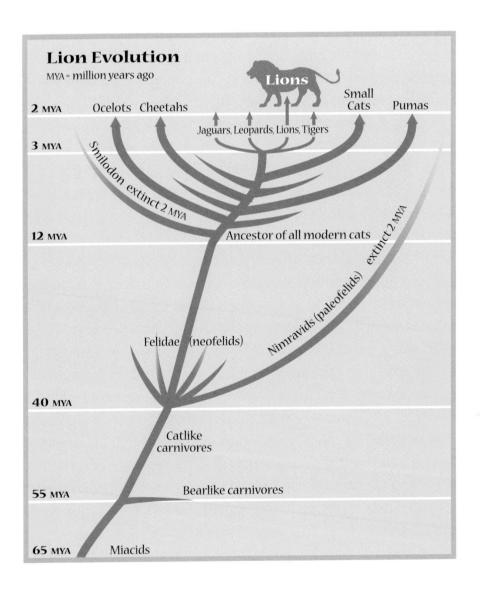

Lion Evolution

MYA = million years ago

2 MYA — Ocelots Cheetahs — **Lions** — Small Cats — Pumas

Jaguars, Leopards, Lions, Tigers

3 MYA

Smilodon extinct 2 MYA

12 MYA — Ancestor of all modern cats

Felidae (neofelids)

Nimravids (paleofelids) extinct 2 MYA

40 MYA

Catlike carnivores

55 MYA — Bearlike carnivores

65 MYA — Miacids

Sometime after three million years ago, one line of neofelids evolved into the ancestors of tigers, leopards, jaguars, and lions.

Paleontologists have found fossils of tigers, jaguars, and leopards dating back to about two million years ago. The oldest fossils recognizable as direct relatives of modern lions, however, are only about 750,000 years old. For this reason paleontologists think that lions are among the youngest of the cat species.

The oldest lion fossils come from West Africa. Lions probably originated there and then spread across Africa, north into Europe, and east into Asia. One large species, *Panthera spelaea*, called the cave lion, lived across Eurasia from England to Siberia. Scientists think that the lions shown in the oldest cave paintings of France and Spain belong to this species.

The clouded leopard, a big cat native to Southeast Asia, is a relative of the lion, although it does not belong to the genus *Panthera*. When lions were more numerous in Asia, their range and that of the clouded leopard sometimes overlapped.

Another lion species migrated from Asia to North America the same way early humans did—by traveling across the Bering land bridge, a land mass that connected Siberia to Alaska during the Ice Age, at a time when ocean levels dropped dramatically. This species evolved into the American lion, *Panthera atrox*, which lived across North America and as far south as Peru in South America. Like the saber-toothed cats, American lions sometimes fell victim to the La Brea Tar Pits. Fossils recovered from the pits show that American lions were similar to modern African lions, but about 25 percent larger.

Between 100,000 and 10,000 years ago, changes in climate and environmental conditions drove lions to extinction in the Americas and most of Europe. The sole surviving species, *Panthera leo*, was left in possession of Africa, southern and eastern Europe, and western and southern Asia. It is this lion that still lives on today in Africa and a tiny corner of Asia.

Modern Subspecies and Their Ranges

Scientists arrange living things into groups using a system called taxonomy, which classifies organisms together by shared features. Taxonomic classification begins with very large groups, called kingdoms. From there it moves through many categories, each more limited than the one above it. At the end of the process is the species—*Panthera leo*, in the case of lions.

Biologists using taxonomic classification place the lion in the following categories:

Kingdom: Animalia (all animals)
Phylum: Chordata (all animals with backbones)
Class: Mammalia (all mammals)
Order: Carnivora (all carnivores)

Family: Felidae (all cats)
Subfamily: Pantherinae (lions, tiger, jaguars, leopards, snow
    leopards, clouded leopards, and marbled cats)
Genus: *Panthera* (lions, tigers, leopards, jaguars, snow leopards*)
Species: *leo*

*Some taxonomists place snow leopards in a separate genus.

    There is only one lion species, but it is divided into varieties
called subspecies. A subspecies is a population that is recognizably
different from the other members of its species. Although members of separate subspecies can interbreed, the subspecies usually

The Lion's Body

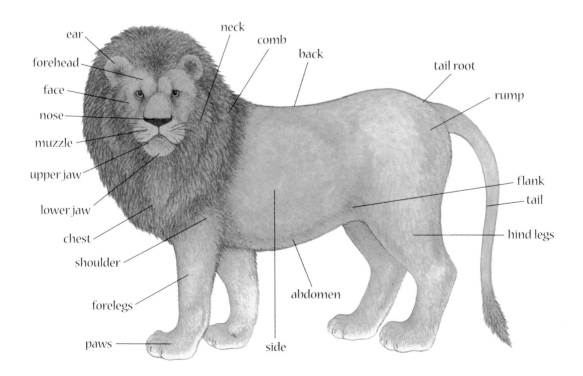

live in different regions. Because they are somewhat isolated from each other, they remain distinct rather than merging into a single population through interbreeding. Where the ranges of two subspecies overlap slightly, they interbreed, but a small amount of interbreeding is not enough to overwhelm their differences.

Biologists frequently disagree about subspecies. When they study a particular population of plants or animals, some are likely to argue that it forms a distinct subspecies (or even a species), while others claim that it is simply part of the main species. Although experts agree that all modern lions belong to the same species, lists of lion subspecies vary greatly. Some observers try to recognize as many varieties as possible, while others prefer to make fewer distinctions. The issue is not just scientific, it is also related to politics and conservation. Some people feel that if regional or local populations of lions are recognized as distinct subspecies, they will receive higher standards of protection under environmental laws. In simplest terms, the idea is that a country with two thousand lions might regard its lion population as large and healthy, but if that same country had four different subspecies of lions with only five hundred animals in each sub-species, it might try harder to protect them all.

One subspecies that all experts recognize is *Panthera leo persica*, the Asiatic lion. These lions once inhabited a vast range, from the forested mountains of Greece across Turkey, Iran, and Afghanistan into Pakistan and northern India. Over the centuries, however, Asiatic lions died out in much of their range. Some were killed by hunters. In addition, growing human populations and their activities, such as farming, disturbed the habitats of lions and the wild animals they preyed on.

Two hundred years after lions feasted on the Persian emperor's baggage camels in Macedonia, the Greek philosopher Aristotle wrote that lions had become rare in Greece and the surrounding lands. By the end of the first century C.E. lions had been wiped out in Europe. They still lived in Israel in the twelfth century C.E., at the time of the Crusades, but in the centuries that followed their numbers in the Near East dwindled dramatically. The last known lion in Turkey was killed in 1870, the last in Iraq was killed in 1918, and no lions have been sighted

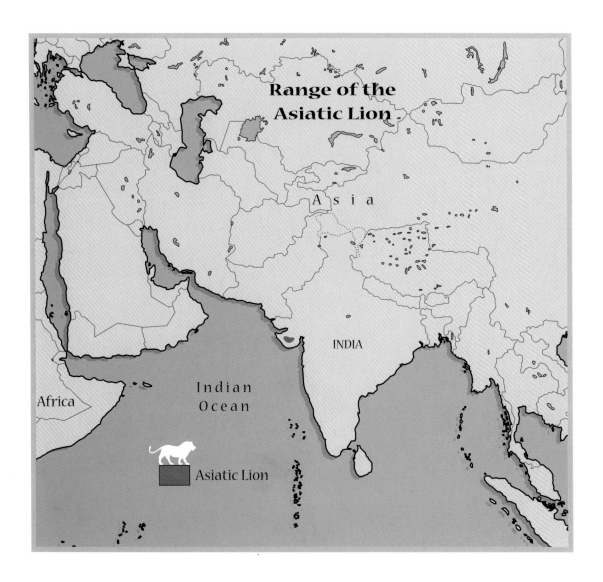

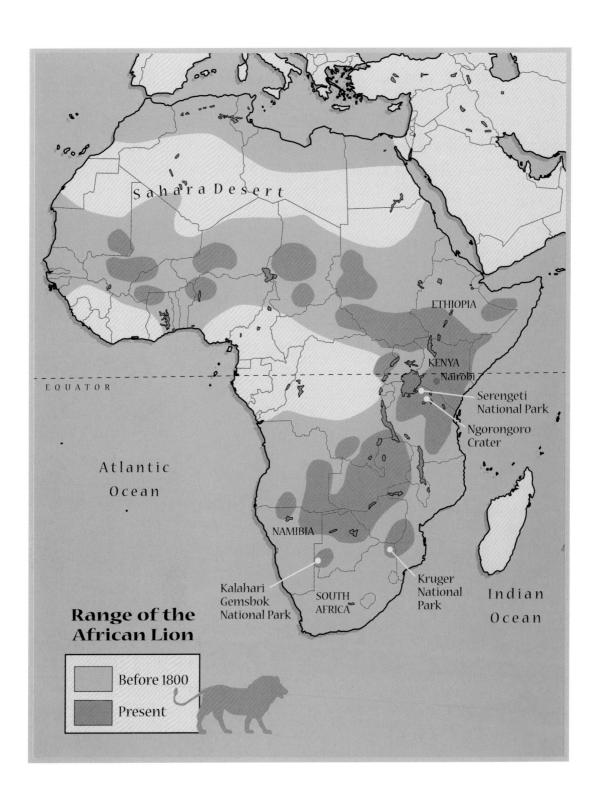

S a h a r a   D e s e r t

ETHIOPIA

KENYA

Nairobi

Serengeti
National Park

Ngorongoro
Crater

EQUATOR

Atlantic
Ocean

NAMIBIA

Kalahari
Gemsbok
National Park

SOUTH
AFRICA

Kruger
National
Park

Indian
Ocean

**Range of the
African Lion**

Before 1800

Present

in Iran since 1942. Lions were exterminated in Pakistan even earlier, by 1810, partly because British army officers and government officials hunted them avidly. They also hunted lions enthusiastically in India. They killed so many (along with tigers) that in 1891 one British scientist observed that "in India the lion is verging on extinction." Yet today India is the one place where the Asiatic lion still exists. A small population of *Panthera leo persica* survives in a protected area in the Gir Forest of northeastern India.

All lions other than the Asiatic lions are African lions. Although DNA tests have revealed small genetic differences between Asiatic lions and African lions, attempts to identify various subspecies of African lions through genetic testing have had mixed results. Relationships among lions can be traced through DNA, but genetic science has not yet shown clear boundaries between the African subspecies. Most scientists now recognize, at most, six subspecies of African lions.

Two of these subspecies became extinct in the wild in recent historical times. The Barbary lion, *Panthera leo leo*, largest of the lions, once lived in North Africa from Morocco to Egypt. Males bore a distinctive, very full mane that was golden-yellow around the face and black behind the face. This mane, running along the length of its belly, covered more of the lion's body than that of other species. The Barbary lion was the lion best known to the ancient Romans, who captured specimens in their African colonies and carried them to Rome for their gladiatorial combats. It was also the first lion to be named and studied by European scientists. Many of the lions that appear in European art from the Renaissance and later periods are Barbary lions. By 1920, however, these impressive beasts had died out in the wild and were believed to be extinct. In recent years a handful of lions with Barbary-style manes have been found in zoos, circuses, and private menageries, such as the wildlife collection of the kings of Morocco. None of these animals were captured in the wild—they are descendants of animals that have lived in captivity for at least several generations. Some researchers, believing that these animals are Barbary lions, at least in part, have begun developing breeding programs aimed at restoring the subspecies. Scientists do not yet know, however, whether these recovered animals are true Barbary lions, or whether enough of the Barbary genetic heritage remains for a meaningful recovery effort.

The Cape lion, *Panthera leo melanochaitus*, was native to the Cape Province of South Africa, the southern tip of the continent.

THE FASTEST OF THE CATS, THE CHEETAH LIVES IN MANY OF THE SAME PARTS OF AFRICA AS THE LION. ALTHOUGH THE TWO BIG CATS SOMETIMES COMPETE FOR THE SAME FOOD, CHEETAHS TEND TO AVOID DIRECT CONFLICT BECAUSE LIONS ARE LARGER AND STRONGER.

It became extinct even before the Barbary lion—by 1860 it had vanished from its former range, with only stuffed skins left behind. As with the Barbary lion, some captive lions may be descended from Cape lions or may carry some of their genes. Most experts suspect, however, that the surviving heritage of the Cape lion—if it exists—is too small for the subspecies to be restored.

Two other generally recognized subspecies of African lions are the Senegalese lion, *Panthera leo senegalensis*, which is native to western Africa, and the Transvaal lion, *Panthera leo krugeri*, which lives in southern Africa. Some classification systems

Snow leopards are native to mountainous areas in Asia. Their coats of fur are much thicker than those of lions, allowing them to live in areas never inhabited by the Asiatic lion.

identify the remaining subspecies as the Masai lion, *Panthera leo massaicus*, found in the eastern African nations of Kenya and Tanzania, and the Angola lion, *Panthera leo bleyenberghi*, found in the central African nations of Angola, Congo, and Zimbabwe. Other taxonomists use the names *P. leo nubica* for the East African lion and *P. leo azandica* for the Angola lion.

The Lion's Kin

Lions' closest relatives are the four other species of large cats in the genus *Panthera*: tigers (Asia), jaguars (Central and South America), leopards (Africa and southern Asia), and snow leopards (mountain ranges in Asia). Slightly less close are two other big cats: the cheetah (which shares much of the lion's range in Africa) and the clouded leopard (found in tropical forests of Southeast Asia).

The thirty other cat species that exist are known as the small cats, although the largest of them, the puma, is as large as some of the big cats. The small cats are set apart from the seven big-cat species by physical features such as a shorter snout and a head that is smaller in relation to the body. The best-known species of small cat is *Felis silvestris*. All domestic cats belong to this species, which also exists in the wild. One wild subspecies, *Felis silvestris libyca*, lives in Africa and occasionally shares the lion's range. So do several other small cats, including the serval and the African golden cat. Lions also overlap with leopards and cheetahs. The fact that all of these animals are cats does not count for anything when they meet, however. All are carnivores, and the larger ones prey on the smaller. As the largest cats in Africa, lions have been known to kill all of the other cat species in their range.

In India tigers are larger than lions, but the two species rarely

THE TIGER AND THE LION ONCE OCCUPIED MUCH THE SAME RANGE IN INDIA AND
OTHER PARTS OF ASIA. TODAY, HOWEVER, THE TWO SPECIES SELDOM MEET BECAUSE
THE BOTH HAVE BECOME RARE. ALTHOUGH TIGERS AND LIONS AVOID ONE ANOTHER
IN THE WILD AND DO NOT INTERBREED, CAPTIVE LIONS AND TIGERS THAT HAVE BEEN
REARED TOGETHER SINCE BIRTH OCCASIONALLY MATE AND PRODUCE HYBRID CUBS.

The Asiatic lion was once found across a wide area, from Greece to India. Today its range has shrunk to a small part of India's Gir Forest, where a park has been set aside as a refuge for the surviving members of the subspecies.

fight because tigers are solitary hunters, while lions generally hunt in groups. In addition, the two species almost never meet because the remaining territory of the Asiatic lion is so small, and both Asiatic lions and tigers are now so rare. Even when they were more numerous in India, they avoided one another and, as separate species, did not interbreed. Yet tigers and lions are related closely enough that in zoos, pairs of lions and tigers that were reared together as cubs have occasionally mated and produced infertile offspring.

3   Basic Biology

I n *Born Free*, Joy Adamson describes a journey with Elsa to a forested mountaintop when the lioness was not yet two years old. Adamson's description shows that a lion's body and senses are beautifully adapted to its habitats and to its life as a hunter. After telling how easily Elsa climbed the steep, rocky trail, she wrote:

> *Because of the shade and altitude, walking during the heat of the day was no effort in this region, and [Elsa] was able to explore the mountain with us. She watched the eagles circling high in the air and was annoyed by the crows who followed her and dived low to tease her, and on one occasion she woke a buffalo out of his sleep and chased him. She had*

THE WHISKERS ON A LION'S CHIN, EYEBROWS, AND CHEEKS ARE SENSITIVE ORGANS OF TOUCH. HIGHLY SENSITIVE WHISKERS ALSO GROW FROM DARK SPOTS ON EITHER SIDE OF THE NOSE. THOSE SPOTS FORM A PATTERN THAT IS UNIQUE TO EACH LION, LIKE A HUMAN FINGERPRINT.

excellent scent, hearing, and eyesight and never lost herself in the thick undergrowth. One afternoon . . . Elsa was ambushing us playfully from behind every bush, when suddenly, from the direction in which she had just disappeared, we heard a panic-stricken bray. A moment later a donkey broke through the wood with Elsa clinging to it and mauling it.

The Adamsons rescued the terrified donkey, which was part of their train of pack animals, but they were impressed by Elsa's first display of a hunting instinct. They were reminded that she shared the physical features, keen senses, and killer instincts that make lions feared and respected as predators.

Physical Features

Lions are the second largest cats, after tigers. Their size, however, varies considerably. Not only is there a wide range of body sizes among wild lions, but captive lions are generally larger, on average, than wild ones.

Adult male lions weigh between 330 and 550 pounds (150 and 250 kg). They typically measure 5.5 to 8 feet (1.7 to 2.5 m) from the tip of the nose to the base of the tail, with an additional 3 feet (1 m) or so of length in the tail. Females are smaller on average, weighing 265 to 400 pounds (120 to 181 kg). Their head-and-body length is 4.5 to 6 feet (1.4 to 1.8 m), and their tails are 2 to 3 feet (0.7 to 1 m) long.

Size is not the only difference in appearance between lions and lionesses. The lion species is the only cat species in which males and females show an obvious difference in physical characteristics—a condition that biologists call sexual dimorphism. The lion's sexual dimorphism concerns its most widely recognized feature: its mane. Lions have a mane, except in a few

A LION IS SUPERBLY ADAPTED TO ITS LIFE AS A HUNTER AND CARNIVORE. ITS PAWS HOUSE LETHAL CLAWS, AND ITS TONGUE IS COVERED WITH FLESHY SPIKES THAT ARE USEFUL FOR GROOMING ITS FUR AND ALSO HELP STRIP THE FLESH OF PREY FROM THE BONES.

small population subgroups, such as the maneless lions of Selous Game Reserve in Tanzania. Lionesses, however, never have a mane. The size and fullness of a lion's mane varies and so does

Lion Skull

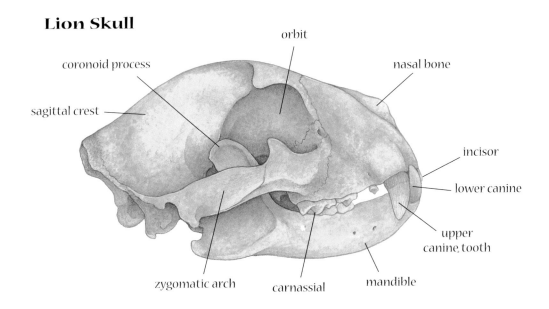

orbit

coronoid process

nasal bone

sagittal crest

incisor

lower canine

upper canine, tooth

zygomatic arch   carnassial   mandible

the color, which tends to darken as the lion ages. Most are yellowish brown in color, but some are reddish or silvery gray, and some are dark brown, almost black. A lion's mane serves two purposes. It offers a layer of padding that protects the throat and neck in fights, especially when it is fighting with other lions, which always strike at the neck. The mane also helps the lion attract mates. Some studies suggest that lionesses prefer partners with larger manes.

The lion's coat, like its mane, varies in color. The most common colors are light tawny or sandy brown, tan, and yellowish gold. Some lions are very pale beige or yellow or even silvery gray. In allowing the animals to blend into their backgrounds of brushy grassland, semidesert, or open woodland, all of these colors provide some degree of camouflage. Occasionally, white lions are born. Some are albinos, animals that lack pigmentation and have reddish eyes (albinism occurs rarely in all animals, not just lions). Others have white coats but eyes of the normal golden amber color. They are leucistic; that is, they suffer from a near-complete absence of normal pigmentation, the same genetic mutation that causes white tigers. Because of their lack of camouflage coloring, neither albino nor leucistic lions are likely to live long in the wild—it is difficult for these cats to sneak up on their prey or to avoid their enemies. Black lions that have been reported are really lions that are very dark brown in color. A lion's coat color is generally lighter on the belly and the insides of the legs than on the upper surfaces of its body. The under-parts may be beige, pale yellow, or white. The color of the back of their ears, in contrast, is often darker than the coat, some-times appearing almost black.

The mane is not the only long hair on the lion's body. Both male and female lions have a tuft of long hair at the end of their tails—a feature not found on any other cat species. The tail tuft is generally darker than the lion's coat, and it sometimes con-tains a small spike or spur of bone that is separate from the bones of the tail. Scientists do not know the purpose of this tail spur, which does not occur in all lions.

Certain physical features are associated with the various lion subspecies. The main feature of the Barbary lion was its thick, dark mane, which extended over the shoulders, part of the back, and the belly. Barbary lions were also stockier and heavier than the average lions of other subspecies. The Cape lion also had a heavy, dark mane that extended to its belly. Transvaal lions are, on average, slightly larger than other living subspecies, and dark manes are more common among them than among other groups. Senegalese lions often have a light-colored coat and a small, light mane, while the Masai lion is slender and may have faint spots on its coat. The Asiatic lion tends to have a long body and a short mane that does not hide its ears (although the mane of these lions sometimes grows longer and fuller in captivity, for unknown reasons). The Asiatic lion also has a belly fold, a flap or a fold of skin that runs along the length of its belly. Some African lions, however, also have a belly fold. When it comes to physical features, there are no hard-and-fast rules for telling one subspecies from another. Distinctive features may be seen in the general subspecies population, but variations among individual lions are great enough that a lion in any subspecies can look much like a lion in any other group.

A Lion's Body

Lions are marvels of power, strength, and grace in motion. They owe their success as hunters to their skeleton and muscles. A lion's spine—the chain of bones that runs from the base of its head to the tip of its tail—is very flexible, able to twist and turn easily. The animal can sink its body low to the ground and stalk its prey in a crouching crawl. It can arch its spine high, with hind paws pulled close to forepaws, to coil itself like a spring for a powerful leap. And it can twist in midair to change direction or snatch at its fleeing prey.

Although lions are heavily muscled all over their body, they have especially strong muscles in their hind legs and in their neck. The hind legs provide plenty of power for explosive movements, such as jumping—a lion can jump to heights of more than 12 feet (4 m) or spring forward across distances of up to 40 feet (12 m). These strong muscles also drive the animal forward when it runs. Lions can reach a speed of up to 40 miles (64 km) per hour. Lions are not designed for long-distance running, however. Their legs and feet are better suited to springing and sprinting than to steady trotting or galloping, and their lungs are too small in relation to their body size to provide enough oxygen for sustained running, so lions move at high speeds only

Lion Skeleton

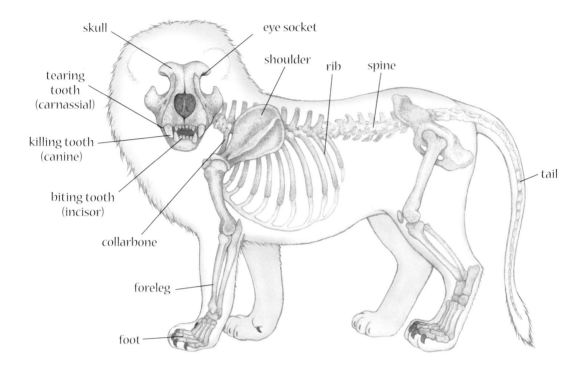

skull

eye socket

shoulder

rib

spine

tearing
tooth
(carnassial)

killing tooth
(canine)

biting tooth
(incisor)

collarbone

foreleg

foot

tail

for relatively short distances. The sturdy musculature of a lion's neck helps it tighten its jaws, grip animals larger than itself, and pull the seized prey down.

Lions are good climbers and frequently go into trees, although they cannot climb to great heights because the smaller branches cannot support their weight. A lion may climb a tree for shade, to rest, or to retreat from a threat. Usually, however, it will go no higher than about 20 feet (6.6 m), and it will generally jump down because its backward-curving claws are better suited for traveling up a tree trunk than for climbing down.

Like other cats, lions are digitigrade walkers. This means they walk on their toes rather than on their entire foot, as plantigrade walkers (such as humans) do. A lion's paws are nothing more than its toes, while its lower leg is actually made up of the other foot bones. A thick, bare, fleshy pad across the bottom of the toes provides cushioning and protection, while smaller pads do the same thing for each toe tip. These pads give the lion its pugmark, or footprint: an oval indentation with smaller ovals in front of it. Each toe ends in a sharp, curved claw. Unlike dogs, whose claws are always visible, cats have retractable claws. The claws are normally housed in sheaths or casings inside the pads, but when the lion tightens special tendons in its feet, the claws emerge for use in hunting, fighting, or climbing. Lions have four toes on each hind paw and five on each forepaw. The fifth toe on the forepaw is called a dewclaw and does not touch the ground. Lions use their dewclaws when climbing or gripping.

Lion Paw

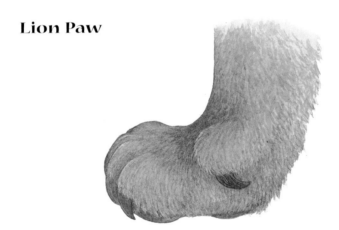

Claws are only part of a lion's weaponry. The lion also has the teeth of a predator. Canine teeth, the long fangs at the upper and lower corners of the jaws, are for stabbing. Carnassial teeth cut and tear. Lions have no chewing teeth—they swallow whole chunks torn from the carcasses of their prey. Like other cats large and small, lions are to some extent dependent on the

Like the earliest known carnivores millions of years ago, lions have carnassial teeth—the bladelike teeth along the sides of the mouth that are ideal for tearing flesh. The longer fangs at the upper and lower front corners are the canine teeth, used for stabbing. A lion's neck and jaw muscles are so strong that the animal can sometimes bite through the spine or leg bone of its prey.

health of their teeth. A lion that breaks its fangs or has infected teeth must turn to prey that is fairly easy to catch and cannot defend itself vigorously, such as humans. Many of the lions that people have destroyed as so-called man-eaters have been lions with dental problems. If a lion's dental problems become too severe, even easy prey or the carcasses of dead animals will be beyond its ability to eat, and it will starve.

Lions, tigers, leopards, snow leopards, and jaguars are sometimes grouped together as the roaring cats (cheetahs, clouded leopards, and small cats are the purring cats). Beneath the tongue of every felid is a set of bones called the hyoid structure. In the purring cats, this structure is stiff. In the roaring cats, two of the hyoid bones are linked by a flexible, stretchy piece of cartilage that enables the cat to enlarge its air passages and expel a large volume of air at once. The deep, coughing roar that emerges is one of the loudest, most impressive sounds in the animal world.

Internally, lions have the same anatomical systems as other mammals. The circulatory system of heart and blood vessels carries blood throughout the body. The respiratory system, consisting of the trachea, or windpipe, and the lungs, infuses the blood with oxygen and removes carbon dioxide, the waste product of breathing. The digestive system consists of the gullet, or throat, the stomach, and the intestines. Liquid waste from the kidneys passes through the bladder before leaving the body as urine, while solid waste, left over from the process of digestion, is expelled through the anus at the end of the digestive system. The male reproductive system consists of testes, which produce and store sperm cells and a penis for delivering the sperm into a female's reproductive tract. In females, ovaries produce eggs that, when fertilized by sperm, develop into fetuses in the lioness's uterus. Like all female mammals, lionesses have

Lion Organs

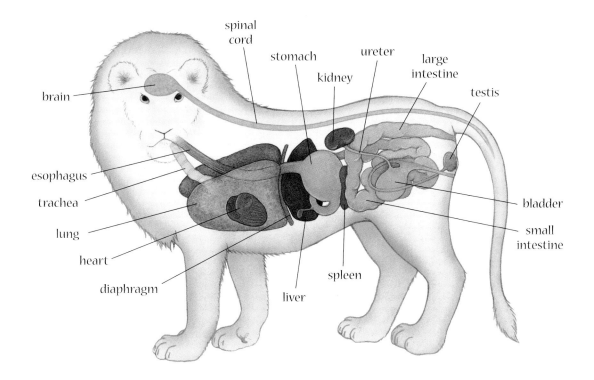

brain

spinal
cord

stomach

kidney

ureter

large
intestine

testis

esophagus

trachea

lung

heart

diaphragm

liver

spleen

bladder

small
intestine

milk-producing glands for suckling their young. A lioness has four mammary glands with nipples arranged along the belly.

Sensing the World

Sight is a lion's most important sense—the animal relies on it more than on hearing or smell to locate its prey. Lions are both diurnal and nocturnal, which means that they are active both by day and night. They cannot see in complete darkness, but they can see at low-light levels that would be impossibly dark to human eyes. A lion's pupil (the opening through which light enters the eye) can enlarge to more than four times the diameter of a human pupil, and so allows the lion to gather more visual information at night. In addition, lions share a feature with all cats and many other nocturnal animals as well: the tapetum lucidum, a shiny membrane that lines the back of a lion's eyes. Light entering the eye is reflected from the membrane and so fills the eye with more light and increases the lion's visual power. (Lions' eyes appear to glow when light falls on them at night because of this membrane.) Like humans and many other animals, lions have binocular vision: the fields of vision from their two eyes overlap, a feature that lets them judge distances accurately without turning their heads.

Hearing is the second most important sense for lions. Wildlife biologists do not know exactly how sharp a lion's hearing is. Some believe that lions may not hear much better than human beings. Like all mammals, lions have fleshy outer ears called pinnae, which capture sound waves and direct them to the inner ear. Unlike humans, though, lions can swivel or rotate the pinnae separately. They use these flexible outer ears to adjust their hearing to different circumstances. To hear sounds from all sides, a lion points its pinnae in different directions. When it is time to zero in on a particular sound, such as the rustle of a zebra moving

LIONS ARE TOP PREDATORS, WHICH IS ONE REASON PEOPLE HAVE CALLED THE LION "THE KING OF BEASTS." ANOTHER REASON IS THE LION'S APPEARANCE, WHICH CAN SEEM TO SUGGEST SUCH QUALITIES AS DIGNITY AND NOBILITY IN ADDITION TO STRENGTH.

through dry grass or the yelps of a hyena pack, a lion points both pinnae at the sound to help it pinpoint direction.

Lions do not track their prey by scent; they locate their prey with sight and sound. They use their sense of smell mainly in their social interactions with other lions. Each lion produces a distinctive personal scent that is present in its urine, its feces, and the liquid from special scent glands in the face, toes, and base of the tail. Lions mark their territory with their own scent by urinating and defecating, rubbing against trees and rocks, and scratching trees. Their sense of scent allows lions to recognize the scent-marked territories of other lions. Like many mammal species, lions and other cats can improve their ability to identify scent through a behavior called flehmen breathing, a kind of super smelling through the mouth. During flehmen breathing, the lion drops its jaw, wrinkles its nose, and sucks in air, which passes over a cluster of cells in the roof of the lion's mouth. These cells, called the vomeronasal organ, allow the lion to pick up chemical clues in another lion's scent.

Covered with taste buds, the tongue is another sense organ. A lion's tongue also has small, fleshy spikes called papillae. Lions use their tongue like a brush to groom their fur and the fur of their young. They also clean wounds with their tongue. Around the lion's mouth are many organs of touch—the stiff hairs called vibrassae, or whiskers. Above the eyes are the superciliary whiskers, on the upper lip at the sides of the nose are the mystacial whiskers, and on the cheeks are the genial whiskers. The longest and most sensitive are the mystacial whiskers. Lions move these long, flexible bristles flat against the sides of their face when they are eating or grooming. Their ability to rotate their whiskers forward into a fan may help them sense objects in front of them, especially at night. Each whisker grows from a dark spot on the lion's face. Wildlife researchers have found that

CLAWING TREE TRUNKS SERVES SEVERAL PURPOSES. IN ADDITION TO SHARPENING THE LION'S CLAWS, IT MARKS THE LION'S TERRITORY IN TWO WAYS: WITH VISIBLE SCRATCHES ON THE TREE AND WITH SCENT FROM GLANDS IN THE LION'S PAWS.

the arrangement of these whisker spots is highly individual, almost like a fingerprint. Scientists observing wild lions have learned to identify particular animals by their whisker spots.

4 A Pride of Lions

Lions are the only social cats. In other cat species, although males and females come together to mate and mothers and their offspring remain together for a while, adult cats are more or less alone in the world. There are a few exceptions. Among the big cats, cheetahs and tigers occasionally form casual, temporary groups when they share feeding grounds or water sources. Among the small cats, feral house cats sometimes gather in loose associations called colonies. Most of the time, though, a cat's life is a solitary one.

Lions live in social networks with their own kind. Each lion is born into an extended family group called a pride, which occupies a specific territory. Some lions remain in their birth pride for their entire life, while others move from pride to pride. Even lions that live on their own—almost always males—once belonged to a pride and are looking for a chance to join a new one. A pride's size and the size of its territory are determined by

PRIDE MEMBERS LOOK ON AS A LIONESS BRINGS DOWN A WILDEBEEST—ONE OF THE LION'S FAVORITE PREY ANIMALS.

features of its habitat. Where prey is abundant, prides tend to be larger and their territories smaller than they are where prey is scarce and hunting is difficult.

Habitats

Asiatic lions once lived in a wide range of habitats, from forests to grassy plains to semidesert scrublands. Today they are found only in one habitat and one place, the Gir Forest. In Africa, however, lions still live in a wide variety of environments. They inhabit the marshy delta of the Okavango River in Botswana and the dry, sparsely vegetated Kalahari Desert of southwestern Africa. They are found at altitudes of 12,000 feet (3,600 m) on the slopes of Ethiopia's mountains and on the lush, lake-dotted plain inside the extinct volcano known as Ngorongoro Crater in Tanzania.

Lions are most commonly found in grassland sprinkled with rocky hills mixed with open forests. This kind of habitat, called savanna, stretches across much of eastern Africa and parts of northern and southern Africa as well. The savanna's grassy plains are home to herds of the lion's favorite prey, grazing animals such as zebras and antelope. Hills are good locations for the den in which a mother lion gives birth and raises her young. Single trees and patches of open forest, free of dense undergrowth, provide shade from the heat of the day, cover for lions lying in ambush, and branches for resting or for escaping from stampedes.

For savanna-dwelling creatures, the year has two seasons: wet and dry. The wet season generally falls between December and May. Grass grows tall and green, streams and ponds brim with water, and grazing animals—wildebeests, eland (the largest antelope), and zebras—roam the plains in the thousands, feeding on the fresh new growth. During the dry season, grasses turn brown, some watercourses dry up, and many of the grazers

A LION GAZES ACROSS THE VAST PLAIN OF SERENGETI NATIONAL PARK IN TANZANIA, WHERE A MILLION WILDEBEESTS AND TWO HUNDRED THOUSAND ZEBRAS ROAM. THE PARK'S NAME, FROM THE LANGUAGE OF AFRICA'S MASAI PEOPLE, MEANS "PLACE WHERE THE LAND GOES ON FOREVER."

move from the plains into areas of open forest, home to elephants, rhinoceroses, buffalo, and giraffes. Other animals, such as warthogs and gazelles (several varieties of small antelope), stay on the plains, surviving on the tough, withered roots and grasses of the dry season.

Lion prides do not move with the seasons but stay within their established territories. Although lions favor zebras and wildebeests in times of abundance, when times are leaner, they will feed on whatever they can catch, including ostriches, snakes, monkeys, fish, tortoises, and crocodiles. Each pride adjusts its hunting to the amount and kind of prey that is available from one season to the next.

Social Structures

When European explorers and hunters began observing lions in their natural habitat, they soon discovered that these cats live together in groups. At first, observers thought that a lion's mating and living arrangements resembled a simplified, idealized vision of a human family: a male and a female, paired for life, raising their offspring together. As with human families, however, the reality of the lion's family life is more complex and varied than it first appeared.

George Schaller's landmark three-year study of lions in Tanzania's Serengeti National Park during the 1960s was the first research project to identify and track large numbers of individual wild lions over time. Schaller's work showed that lions are social cats and that the core of their social organization is a stable group called the pride. It also showed that lions and lionesses have very different roles and life histories.

The center of each pride is a group of related lionesses—sisters, mothers, daughters, grandmothers, cousins, and aunts. The true identity of the pride rests with these female lions, who may maintain direct blood relationships in the same territory over many generations. A pride may be as small as a single lioness and her young offspring or as large as forty. Most prides number from two to twenty females and cubs, with an average size of about a dozen. Female cubs have a life membership in the pride, unless they choose to leave to start their own pride. Male cubs are part of the pride only until they become adults. At that time they either leave voluntarily or are driven away by the females.

Although kinship is the principal link among lionesses in prides, some observers have found that ties among female lions are flexible, especially when the lionesses do not have young cubs. A lioness may leave her pride for a time and then return. Within a pride, females often form subgroups of two or three lionesses each that hunt and rest on their own. A pride occasionally welcomes a temporary or permanent female newcomer that is not a relative, although this is rare. More often, lionesses drive off any unrelated female who tries to join their pride.

Each pride includes one or more male lions, but the males are temporary guests, not permanent members. Sometimes a pride has a single male, but there are usually two to five males, depending upon the size of the pride. These males are almost always related—they are brothers, fathers and sons, or cousins that were born into the same pride. They have left their birth pride and won the right to join the lionesses of a different pride by defeating or scaring off the males that were there before. Occasionally the lionesses in a pride will drive off their males and invite a new band to move in. If food becomes extremely scarce or if the pride loses its young lionesses, the males may leave on their own, looking for better prospects. Generally, however, a lion fights to keep control of his pride and leaves only when another male forces him out. A male or band of males usually

holds on to a pride for only two to four years before younger, more aggressive lions take over.

The takeover of a pride can be a violent spectacle. It seldom happens overnight—in fact, it may play out over weeks. A nomadic lion or group of lions often targets a pride that is defended by only one adult male, or a pride whose defenders are old, sick, or injured. Sometimes, however, the attackers and the defenders are evenly matched lions in their prime. Either way, the incoming lion or coalition prowls the edges of the pride's territory, leaving scent marks and roaring, letting the pride and its defenders know that a showdown is brewing. The newcomers become bolder, invading the territory. At this point the defending male or males may simply depart to avoid a confrontation. Most of the time, they try to hold on to their claims. Eventually the two lions or teams of lions come into direct contact. The fight that results may consist mostly of hissing, snarling, charging, and posturing, with the loser eventually slinking off in defeat. It may also turn into a bloody free-for-all, a savage battle that will end in the death of one or more lions. Either the attackers carry the day or the defenders manage to drive them off. Either way, a dominant male or band of males is left in charge.

Biologists have developed the theory of kin selection to explain why some animals form social groups. According to this theory, lions in a pride cooperate and help each other because they are closely related. Any lion who breeds and raises young

LIONESSES GROOMING. FEMALES, USUALLY RELATED,
FORM THE CORE OF EACH PRIDE. MALES ARE
TEMPORARY MEMBERS.

Relationships among lions are shaped by dominance, an individual's place in the pride's pecking order. A lion that flattens itself on the ground or shows its belly is displaying submission—acknowledging the greater dominance of the standing lion.

has succeeded in passing on genetic material that is connected to all the others. For example, sister lionesses share their kills and even nurse each other's young. Because sisters share many of the same genes, helping a niece or nephew survive is the next best thing to having one's own offspring survive. The theory of kin selection also explains why males in a pride do not fight with each other for the right to mate with the females. Because the males are so often related, the breeding success of any of them passes along some of the genetic heritage of all of them. The females in a pride share one set of genes, and the males share another set. There are no senior males or females with first claim to breeding rights—any male in the pride may mate with any female in it. The primary instinct of a pride's males is to defend these breeding rights and keep other, unrelated lions from mating with their females.

The theory of kin selection also explains why, when new males have taken over a pride, one of their first acts is to try to kill all or most of the young cubs. If the new males succeed in doing so, they will not waste any energy or time protecting cubs that do not carry their own genes. When cubs die, the lionesses will soon become ready to mate again. The pride's new males will mate with the lionesses as soon as possible and father a new set of cubs of their own. Not all lionesses, however, let the new male or males harm their cubs. Some fight to protect the cubs, or hide them until the newcomers are more relaxed around pride members. Lionesses also mate with new males, even when they are not able to become pregnant. Scientists think that this makes the males less aggressive and also confuses them about who is the father of the females' young.

A pride is not a lion's only social group. Male lions that do not belong to a pride are called nomads. Whether they are young males that have recently left their birth pride or older males that have been driven out of a pride, they move about looking for a new group of females to join. Generally a pair or small group of related males stays together during this transition period. The group they form is called a nomad coalition. Another kind of coalition consists of unrelated individuals that band together to travel and hunt. If a coalition of unrelated males succeeds in winning control of a pride, the males will often act as if they are related, sharing breeding rights and protecting one another's cubs. Not all nomads belong to a coalition. Some wandering males are solitary, either by choice or because the other lions in their coalitions have been killed or died for other reasons.

Members of a pride spend a considerable amount of time apart, alone, or in smaller subgroups. These subgroups change over time as partnerships appear to form or break up. Although all members of a pride recognize each other as part of a shared community and territory, they do not always gather in the same place at the same time. Within a pride, the lionesses rear the cubs and do most of the hunting. Males have two responsibilities—to father cubs and to help defend the pride and its territory from enemies, including other lions.

Territory

Each pride maintains a territory in which it hunts and raises its young. A territory must be large enough to provide food and water for the pride. It may be as small as 15 square miles (40 km²) or as large as 150 square miles (400 km²), depending upon the habitat and the amount of game. A pride moves about its territory in search of water, food, or relief from unpleasant conditions, such as heat or insect pests. It does not maintain a permanent nest or center of operations. The only exception occurs when a lioness is ready to give birth. She finds a sheltered spot such as a cave, a rock overhang, or a clearing inside a thicket. A lioness keeps her newborn young in this den for more than a month, and during this time their pride mates may remain close at hand. Often, in fact, two or more lionesses are denning at the same time.

Pride members do not always remain together in the same part of the territory. When a pride is large, its members may hunt or rest as much as 10 miles (16 km) apart. Lionesses move about less than males. In a twenty-four-hour period, a lioness may travel only 3 miles (5 km) or so while hunting. Males, however, roam over greater distances, because it is to their benefit and that of their cubs to patrol and protect the borders of the pride's territory.

Pride borders sometimes shift over time as prides grow larger or smaller, stronger or weaker. In addition, the territories of two prides may overlap. If so, animals from the different prides generally try to avoid one another. Sometimes, though, prides encounter each other directly, such as when both are following a large herd of grazing animals or resting near a water source. Many of these encounters are peaceful, especially if the lions in both groups are well fed.

Lions also share their territory with a variety of other predators, including other big cats. Although lions kill cheetahs when they can catch them, cheetahs usually manage to outrun lions. And because cheetahs tend to hunt in the middle of the day, when lions are generally resting, encounters are not common. Lions in woodland areas sometimes cross paths with leopards. A leopard will usually try to escape from a lion by fleeing to a high tree branch. If it cannot do so, the lion may kill it, or the two may fight and then go their separate ways.

The lion's most violent interactions are with the spotted hyena. A single lion has little to fear from a single hyena—if the

The pride tears at a fallen impala. Tension and competition among pride members reach a peak when lions gather over a kill.

two fight, the lion will easily kill the hyena. But hyenas tend to hunt in large packs, and they are bold and quick. They prefer to scavenge food when they can, and they are frequent scavengers at a lion's kill, just as lions often scavenge hyenas' kills. Hyena packs also attack and kill lions.

Communication

Male lions use scent and sound to warn possible rivals or enemies away from their territory. They mark their territorial borders with strong-smelling urine and scent from their scent glands. This conveys an unmistakable message to other lions: "This territory is taken. Enter at your own risk." They also roar. A lion's roar travels through the air for several miles (or kilometers), announcing the animal's presence both to the members of its own pride and to outsiders. It warns away leonine invaders and other animals, such as elephants, which might cause trouble if they stumbled into the pride. Lions also scratch the ground and the trunks of trees, leaving visible marks and deposits from scent glands in their paws. Like roars and urine sprays, these signs are warnings to outsiders.

Scent and sound are also used for communication within the pride. Each lion recognizes the distinctive personal scent of all its pride mates. When pride members meet, they often spend some time rubbing their head or paws on each other, licking each other's face or body, and smelling each other. These greeting rituals help the lions recognize one another and strengthen the bonds among pride members.

Lions and other roaring cats cannot purr, but they can and do make many other feline noises. They meow, hiss, and snarl. Such sounds are generally accompanied by body language that all lions readily recognize. Ears flattened back against the head

GROOMING AND HEAD-RUBBING STRENGTHEN TIES AMONG PRIDE MEMBERS. SUCH GESTURES OCCUR MOST OFTEN BETWEEN TWO RELATED FEMALES OR BETWEEN A MATING PAIR, BUT SOMETIMES THEY OCCUR BETWEEN TWO MALES, AS HERE.

are a sign of anger and aggression—the lion is getting its ears out of the way in case the claws start flying. Eyes narrowed to slits are another protective gesture that often signals a readiness to fight or attack. A lion that wants to avoid conflict crouches low to the ground and may roll onto its back, while a lion that feels more dominant holds its head high and may bristle its mane and raise its tail. Lions often roar at night. Biologists think that they use sound to keep in touch when they cannot see one another because of darkness or because they have become separated, and also to warn off nocturnal predators.

PRIDE MEMBERS SLEEPING TOGETHER. SPOTS SIMILAR TO THOSE OF LEOPARDS ARE VISIBLE ON SOME OF THE YOUNGER ANIMALS. THESE SPOTS ALMOST ALWAYS DISAPPEAR AS THE LIONS MATURE.

Feeding

Although lions are carnivores and predators, they spend as little time hunting as possible. They typically sleep or rest for about eighteen to twenty hours a day. The rest of their time is spent interacting with pride members, patrolling territorial borders, and feeding.

A lion may get a meal by scavenging or hunting. Scavenging means finding and eating animals that are already dead—for example, locating the carcass of an animal that has died of old age, injury, or illness. Often, though, it means finding prey that some other predator has killed and taking it away from the hunter. Lions scavenge the kills of hyenas and jackals, as well as other cats—cheetahs, leopards, and other lions. Such scavenging may seem unsportsmanlike and unworthy of the king and queen of beasts, but hunting is a difficult business. It takes a lot of energy and often fails to get results. Scavenging is an efficient way to get food by spending relatively small amounts of energy. As much as 50 percent of a lion's food may be scavenged. Lions, in turn, have their own kills scavenged by other lions, jackals, hyenas, vultures, and other predators that dart in to tear a mouthful from the carcass of the prey that a lion has brought down.

Lions hunt either by day or by night, whenever prey is available and they are hungry. Most of the time, though, they prefer to hunt at dawn or dusk. Both male and female lions hunt individually and in groups, but in any pride, lionesses tend to make more kills than lions do. When hunting alone, a lioness is likely to go after small gazelles and warthogs, although a single lion can bring down prey up to twice his or her weight. But when two or more lionesses are hunting together, they generally target larger prey such as zebras and wildebeests because these animals offer more food per kill. By hunting together, they can bring down prey that weighs more than four times as much as a lion, such as a buffalo or an elephant calf.

Lions' preferred prey, zebras and wildebeests, can outrun even the fastest lion, so lions rarely try to chase prey over distances. Instead, they use the methods of stalking and ambush. When stalking, lions or lionesses creep very slowly and stealthily toward their intended prey. If possible, they stalk animals that have become isolated from their herd. Old, sick, injured, pregnant, and young animals are especially desirable as prey because they cannot run as fast as healthy adults and are easier to bring down. Sometimes the lion focuses on a specific target for a long time, slinking closer bit by bit while using tall grass and trees or bushes as cover. In other cases the lion may stalk a whole group of animals and then make a sudden dart and try to pick off any individual who panics and becomes separated from the rest. When lions or lionesses are hunting together, they stalk the prey from several different directions. As many as six or eight lionesses may join together in a communal or cooperative hunt. The ambush method of hunting allows lions to save their energy for the final quick attack. Ambushing prey involves lying quiet and concealed, waiting for unsuspecting prey to pass close by. Good places for ambush are along trails leading to water, along trails through thorny thickets or areas of dense brush, and on overhanging rocks or tree limbs.

Once the prey is within reach, a lion strikes quickly, pouncing or chasing, counting on surprise. A lion may throw itself onto the back of a small prey animal or even knock the prey to the ground with a single blow from its mighty clawed paw. With larger prey, however, lions generally leap at the neck or head. An attacking lion tries to sink its teeth into the prey's throat or bite its mouth. Either move will prevent the prey from breathing, making it helpless. In communal hunts, the first attacker aims at the throat or face, while the other lionesses attack the hindquarters and the underbelly. But even experienced hunters miss their prey far more often than they catch it. A pack of hunting lionesses may have to stalk a dozen animals to bring one down, while a lion or lioness hunting alone may miss seventeen or eighteen times for every kill.

Tension within a pride reaches its highest point right after a kill. The easygoing equality of everyday life and the cooperation of the hunt disappear in the competition to consume the carcass. The stronger members of the pride shoulder the weaker ones aside. Males may crowd females out, even when the

females have done the hunting. Adults snarl at youngsters, warning them to keep away. Younger, smaller, weaker lions rarely have the opportunity to feast freely—they usually have to content themselves with quick bites snatched on the run when they dart in between their more powerful pride mates or with scraps left over after the more dominant animals have had their fill. Cubs who are too hungry to wait may try to force their way in to the carcass among the feeding adults. If so, they are likely to get swatted and may even be mauled or killed.

Lions do not hunt or eat every day and may go for several days or even a week without feeding. Their digestive system is designed to handle a large amount of meat in a single meal, so when they do find or catch prey, they tend to devour it all within a short time. A male lion can eat up to 75 pounds (34 kg) in one meal, a female slightly less. One good feeding can turn a gaunt, hungry lion into a plump, satisfied individual who will spend the next week resting and digesting.

UNLESS IT IS VERY OLD, VERY YOUNG, OR SICK, A ZEBRA CAN OUTRUN A LION. THE LION DOES NOT TRY TO CHASE DOWN ITS PREY OVER A LONG DISTANCE—INSTEAD, IT CREEPS UP STEALTHILY ON THE PREY OR AMBUSHES IT, BREAKING INTO THE OPEN ONLY FOR THE FINAL SHORT PURSUIT. WHEN A LION OR LIONESS HUNTS ALONE, WITHOUT THE HELP OF PRIDE MEMBERS, IT MAY SUCCEED IN BRINGING DOWN ONLY ONE ANIMAL FOR A DOZEN AND A HALF ATTEMPTS.

5 The Leonine Life Cycle

A lion may look relaxed and restful as it dozes under a tree in the heat of the day, but its life is not easy. Hunting fast-moving prey and defending a territory are dangerous and demanding tasks. The life of a top predator is a harsh one, and the majority of wild lions die violently or of starvation. Lions begin facing the challenges of this life as soon as they are born.

Courtship and Mating

The life cycle of a lion begins with the mating of its parents, which takes place when the lioness enters a period of mating readiness called estrus. Estrus can occur at any time of the year and usually lasts for four to six days. Sometimes many or all of the lionesses in a pride enter estrus at the same time, an occurrence called breeding synchrony. It usually happens after the pride has been taken over by a new group of males who have

CUBS IN THE MASAI MARA NATIONAL RESERVE, KENYA. THESE CUBS, CLOSE TOGETHER IN AGE, ARE PROBABLY THE OFFSPRING OF SEVERAL LIONESSES. WHEN LIONESSES GIVE BIRTH WITHIN A FEW MONTHS OF EACH OTHER, THEY RAISE THEIR CUBS TOGETHER IN A GROUP, AND THE YOUNG LIONS REGARD EACH OTHER AS LITTERMATES.

killed the cubs of the previous males. The death of their young triggers the start of a new breeding cycle in the lionesses.

A lioness in estrus gives off a scent that males can readily detect. Even males that are in a remote part of the territory will hurry to her side. They will not fight over the right to mate with her, and she may mate with more than one of them during her estrus. Usually the lioness indicates her choice of mate through courtship behavior. She rubs her head against him and allows him to rub his head against her. The two may walk together making a low, soft, rumbling sound like a muted growl.

When the lioness is ready to mate, she lies on her belly or crouches and raises her tail. The male approaches her from behind—cautiously, because she may change her mind and attack him. The male often grips the female by the back of the neck during mating, perhaps to prevent such a change of mind. The act of mating lasts only a few seconds. As soon as it is over, the lion moves quickly away from the lioness, who is likely to snarl and swat at him if he lingers. After fifteen minutes or so, the pair mate again and continue to do so throughout the lioness's estrus, for a total of perhaps three hundred or more matings.

This sexual marathon is a necessary part of the lion's reproductive cycle. Lionesses are induced ovulators: their ovaries do not release eggs on a regular schedule, as those of female humans and many other animals do, but only when they receive a signal or stimulus. The mating act is the signal that causes the ovaries to release eggs—lionesses are capable of getting pregnant only after repeated matings. A lion whose lionesses are all in estrus at the same time is kept busy for days on end. Some experts estimate that a successful male lion experiences about twenty thousand mating acts during his half dozen or so peak reproductive years.

If a lioness does not become pregnant during her estrus, she enters estrus again in a month or two. Often pregnancy does not occur until after four or five estrus periods. Once she has become pregnant, the lioness will not enter estrus again until she has raised her cubs to the age of about two years—or lost them.

LIONS MATING IN THE MASAI MARA NATIONAL RESERVE, KENYA, START THE PROCESS BY SNIFFING EACH OTHER.

Cubs

A lioness gestates her young, or carries them inside her uterus, for between 100 to 120 days, with an average gestation period of 110 days. A pregnant lioness does not gain a great deal of weight—in fact, a lioness who has just gorged herself on a carcass looks fatter than one who is ready to give birth.

When the time has come for her to bear her cubs, the lioness retreats to her den, which may be the same place she

ZOOKEEPERS AND WILDLIFE BIOLOGISTS HAVE LEARNED THAT ORPHANED LION CUBS MAY SURVIVE WITH A LITTLE HELP FROM NURSING MOTHERS OF OTHER SPECIES. THESE YOUNG CUBS ARE NURSING FROM A MOTHER DOG, ALONG WITH HER PUPPIES.

was born. Lionesses generally use the same den for each litter they bear. A litter may contain only a single cub, but the most common number is three, and some litters consist of two or four cubs. Often in larger litters, one or two cubs are small and weak. These are likely to die in infancy, in which case the lioness raises the remaining two healthy cubs.

As soon as a cub is born, the lioness licks it vigorously not only to clean the newborn but to stimulate it to breathe and to empty its bowels and bladder for the first time. Licking is also the

A LIONESS GROOMS HER CUBS. GROOMING NOT ONLY KEEPS A LION'S COAT CLEAN AND HEALTHY BUT—PERHAPS MORE IMPORTANT—IS A FORM OF COMMUNICATION AND BONDING AMONG FAMILY AND PRIDE MEMBERS.

cub's introduction to grooming, a ritual that lions perform with each other throughout their lives to help keep their fur clean and also to strengthen the bonds between pride members.

Newborn cubs weigh between 2 and 4.5 pounds (1 and 2 kg). Their fur is fluffy and spotted, but usually the spots fade as they mature. The cubs can crawl, but they cannot stand or see. Their eyes are covered with pale blue film, which clears away within three to twelve days. The mother nourishes the cubs with milk from her mammary glands, which will be their only food for the first several months or so of their life. The cubs spend their first few weeks close to their mother, comforted by her familiar smell and warmth. If she leaves them to hunt or feed, they are at great risk of being killed by any predator who happens across the den.

By the time they are a month old, the cubs have gotten their first set of teeth. They can also walk and see, but not very well. They cannot judge distances accurately until they are a couple of months old. Slowly, clumsily at first and then more gracefully, the cubs begin playing, an activity that will continue throughout their early years. They jump, pounce, wrestle, and roll together. They begin to chase things: their mother's tail, a blade of grass stirred by the breeze, a grasshopper. Play helps a young lion develop physically by exercising its body and exciting its nervous system. It also lets the lion develop and practice the skills it will need one day for hunting and fighting.

If the lionesses in a pride are in breeding synchrony, two or more of them may give birth to a litter at around the same time. If the young from different litters are within three months of each other in age, the lionesses raise them in a kind of group nursery that biologists call a crèche. Together, the lionesses look after all of the cubs, and any cub can nurse from any lioness that is producing milk. Communal, or shared, caretaking allows one or two females to remain in charge of the group's cubs while the others hunt. The crèche remains in existence for about eighteen or twenty months, giving cubs a large family of "siblings" as playmates. Cubs raised this way tend to remain close throughout their lives. A lioness will rear her young independently, however, if no other litters are close to hers in age.

Between six and twelve weeks of age, cubs begin to interact with other members of the pride, including males. They no longer remain in the den at all times but begin to follow the pride in its activities. By the time they are two months old, their mother may begin giving them meat, in the form of small scraps or regurgitated food, but they still rely on milk for most of their nutrition.

Play becomes increasingly vigorous during the cubs' first year. They play with each other endlessly, but they also seek play partners among the adult lions. Females are generally tolerant and will gently box or wrestle with cubs. A rested and well-fed male may put up with such activities, but a cub who insists on pestering a tense or nervous adult male is risking rough treatment—a powerful swat or worse. By and large, males tend to ignore their young.

One of the most dangerous times in a cub's life comes at around five or six months of age, when the youngster begins following the pride to the carcass of a kill. Young lions are always hungry and are strongly attracted to blood and meat, but the feeding frenzy around a carcass is no place for the small and weak. If food is plentiful and the lions are well fed, cubs may have no trouble helping themselves to scraps or leftovers. At other times, however, they may be injured or killed when trying to snatch food. Even among siblings, food causes fights—larger cubs grab it away from smaller ones. Lionesses stop nursing cubs when the young are between six and eight months of age, but at

A CUB NIPS AT ANOTHER, OLDER CUB. THROUGH SUCH BEHAVIOR, INCLUDING MOCK FIGHTING, YOUNG LIONS TEST THE SOCIAL BONDS AND LEARN THE RULES OF ACCEPTABLE BEHAVIOR IN THE PRIDE.

that age, cubs are not yet able to kill prey on their own. They are entirely dependent upon scavenging scraps from the pride's meals. If they do not succeed, they starve.

When it is about a year old, a cub begins hunting, usually by following its mother or another adult and imitating its actions. At this time the adult often allows the youngster to share more freely in the pride's kill. By about fifteen months or so, a young lion can generally capture and kill small prey, such as a little gazelle or newborn wildebeest. Most of the time, though, lions

CUBS PLAY WITH FEMALE ADULTS AS PART OF THE GROWING-UP PROCESS.

Scraps from a kill are doled out to hungry cubs. Lions begin eating meat when they are about two months old, and after they stop nursing at about six or eight months of age, they depend entirely on the bites of meat they can snatch from the carcasses.

EVEN WHEN PLAYING, VERY YOUNG CUBS DO NOT LIKE TO BE FAR FROM THEIR MOTHERS. LIONESSES ARE PROTECTIVE AND WILL DEFEND THE CUBS AGAINST HYENAS, JACKALS, OR OTHER POSSIBLE PREDATORS.

of this age help older lionesses in communal hunts. Between two and three years of age, a lion becomes capable of stalking and killing larger prey on its own. At that time maternal care ends. The young lion's mother enters estrus again, if she has not done so already, and begins preparing to raise a new litter. The cub who survives to become an adult is lucky. Wildlife scientists believe that 80 percent or more of all cubs die before reaching adulthood.

Adult Life

Lions enter adulthood at about two or two and a half years of age but do not reach their full size and weight until they are between four and six years old. Females can bear young at two but generally do not do so until several years later. A male's mane usually begins developing in the third year, around the time the lion reaches sexual maturity. Although he is physically able to father offpsring, he probably will not get the chance to do so for another few years.

The onset of sexual maturity brings about a big change in a young male's life—he is driven away from his birth pride, along with other young males of his age. He may be forced out in several ways. If a new band of males takes over the pride, all of the surviving males, mature adults as well as young adults, usually leave together. Often, though, young males are forced out by the senior lions in the pride, including their own parents. If a pride takeover is brewing, young males may leave on their own before the fighting starts.

Newly independent males may roam about for a few years as nomads, often partnered in a coalition with their siblings or related crèche mates. Unrelated males may join forces during this time to form a lasting coalition. By the time the nomads are four or five years old, they are approaching their peak size and strength, and they are ready to claim their own first pride.

Not all males find themselves part of a coalition or a pride. Solitary nomads may become what biologists call satellite males, individuals who hang around just outside the territorial borders of a pride. Satellite males avoid fights and mate with females whenever the dominant males are not around. A lioness in estrus sometimes seeks out a satellite male as a mating partner.

A young male lion driven from a pride can sometimes look forward to resuming social life in a coalition or a new pride. When an older adult lion is defeated or scared away from his pride, however, his future is bleaker. He is already past his physical peak, and his hunting skills and strength have begun to wane. He may be alone, with no coalition partners, or his partners may be equally old. Older male nomads usually live for only a year or two once they have left their last pride. The longest lifespan that a wild male lion can hope for is about eleven years.

Wild lionesses tend to live longer than lions. A lioness is capable of bearing young until the age of thirteen or fourteen. After that time, she may continue to hunt, and when she is no longer effective as a hunter she serves as a caretaker for the cubs of the younger lionesses.

The majority of wild lions meet a violent end. Many are killed by humans, by other lions, or by predators such as hyenas, which frequently attack old or sick lions. Other lions die of injuries inflicted by the hooves or horns of their prey. Lions also die of disease, including rabies and canine distemper, which originate in domestic village dogs and then infect wild jackals, hyenas, and lions. In the 1990s, for example, an outbreak of canine distemper stemming from pet dogs killed more than a thousand lions in Tanzania's Serengeti National Park—a third of

LIONESSES PUT UP WITH A LOT OF ROUGH PLAY BY CUBS. WHEN A CUB GOES TOO FAR, THE LIONESS SNARLS, SNAPS HER TEETH, AND PERHAPS SWATS THE CUB WITH ONE MIGHTY PAW. CUBS THAT ARE TOO RAMBUNCTIOUS OCCASIONALLY MEET HARSHER TREATMENT FROM THE OLDER MALES. MOST OF THE TIME, THOUGH, ADULT MALES IGNORE THE YOUNG.

THESE CUBS WILL BE LUCKY TO REACH MATURITY. A LION'S LIFE IS NOT AN EASY
ONE—WILDLIFE SCIENTISTS ESTIMATE THAT FOUR OF EVERY FIVE LIONS DIE BEFORE
ADULTHOOD.

the park's lion population. Other lions perish from starvation
(especially likely if their teeth are bad) or simple old age. In zoos,
with regular feedings and veterinary care, lions often live for
twenty or more years.

6 The Lion's Future

For much of human history, lions represented the power and majesty of untamed nature. They were among the mightiest and deadliest predators in a dangerous world. Humans, thin-skinned creatures without fangs or claws, huddled in terror around the fire when they heard a lion roar. Killing a lion was something that only kings or the bravest warriors could do.

The relationship between lions and people has changed since ancient times. Lions are still the dangerous predators they have always been, and people who live near them still rightly fear and respect them. But lions are no longer kings who dominate the landscape. Now they depend upon human beings for their very survival.

TOURISTS TAKE PHOTOS OF LION CUBS IN A TANZANIA WILDLIFE CONSERVATION AREA. TODAY, SAFARIS ARE EQUIPPED WITH CAMERAS MORE OFTEN THAN WITH GUNS. IN MANY AFRICAN COUNTRIES, TOURISM—WITH WILDLIFE AS A PRIMARY ATTRACTION—IS A SIGNIFICANT PART OF THE NATIONAL INCOME. CONSERVATIONISTS ARE WORKING TO PROMOTE ENVIRONMENTALLY RESPONSIBLE TOURISM, WHICH MAY BOTH EDUCATE TRAVELERS AND CONTRIBUTE TO THE LONG-TERM WELFARE OF ENDANGERED SPECIES AND HABITATS.

Lions have been driven to extinction over much of the range they occupied just a thousand years ago. Much of the loss has occurred in the last century and a half, caused by two factors: hunting and habitat loss. Thousands upon thousands of lions have been killed by hunters in the past century alone, some as sport trophies, others because they were seen as a threat to people or livestock. Many of the lions that survive today in Africa and all of those in India live in protected parks or preserves, where hunting is banned or at least regulated by law, but these laws are often broken by poachers (illegal hunters). Some African nations have no laws against killing lions outside park borders, while others allow the killing of "problem lions"— a term that can be stretched to cover many situations.

Habitat loss is a more serious threat than hunting. The spread of human farms, roads, and settlements has broken up the large stretches of habitat where lions once lived into small islands, and it continues to nibble away at those islands. Without plains and savannas to support the game animals they prey on, lions cannot survive. The spread of the human population not only chews up wild habitat but also brings lions and people into more direct conflict. When people replace wild lands and zebras with pastures and livestock, lions turn to the livestock as a source of food, with tragic results. Many of the lions killed as pests or even man-eaters were simply trying to survive in their former range.

The International Union for Conservation of Nature (IUCN), an organization that includes wildlife- and wilderness-protection groups from many countries, administers the Convention on International Trade in Endangered Species (CITES), which evaluates the risk of extinction for thousands of species of plants and animals. CITES rates the Asiatic lion as endangered, or at high risk. The African lion is vulnerable, or at risk.

No one knows exactly how many Asiatic lions remain in the wild. A 1990 population count suggested that about 200 of them lived within India's Gir Forest, their only known remaining habitat. Ten years later, biologists estimated the total population at between 200 and 300 animals. The government of India has established the Gir National Park, a 100-square-mile (295 km²) area within the forest, to serve as a sanctuary for the lions. However, the sanctuary is a troubled one. The park is too small to allow the lion population to expand. The forest is not a true wilderness—thousands of people and their livestock also inhabit it, roads cross it, and as many as eighty thousand pilgrims enter it each year to visit temples. With the deer that are their natural prey declining because of habitat loss and competition with cattle, the lions sometimes prey on the livestock of the surrounding villages, and so earn the hostility of local people. In addition, wildlife biologists fear the dangers of keeping all surviving members of the subspecies in a single habitat. An isolated population is at risk for disease or the spread of an unfavorable genetic mutation. Experts would like to establish populations of Asiatic lions in other places, but so far attempts to set aside land and habitat for them have not been successful. The best hope for the Asiatic lion's survival lies in continued protection of the Gir National Park together with carefully managed breeding programs in multiple wild reserves and zoos.

The population of African lions is more difficult to number because it is spread over a much larger area. Since 2000, wildlife researchers have produced estimates of the total African lion population that range from 30,000 to 100,000 or more animals. Most of these lions live under some degree of formal protection, inside a park or preserve. In addition to the threat of poaching, this kind of existence carries potential genetic dangers. If lions (and other wildlife) are confined to safe little

ZOOS SUCH AS THIS ONE IN DHAKA, BANGLADESH, ARE CARRYING OUT BREEDING
PROGRAMS TO PRESERVE THE GENETIC HERITAGE OF BOTH ASIATIC AND AFRICAN
LIONS. SOME WILDLIFE EXPERTS, HOWEVER, QUESTION WHETHER IT IS ENOUGH TO
CONSERVE A SPECIES IN CAPTIVITY WITHOUT SUFFICIENT PROTECTION AND HABITAT
FOR THAT SPECIES TO EXIST IN THE WILD.

"island" habitats, their populations can no longer mix and merge slowly over time, as happens when young males are able to wander from place to place and spread and share their genetic traits. Lions in a confined territory may be forced to inbreed, which means that males may mate with females that are closely related to them. Over time, inbreeding weakens a population by reducing its genetic variability, and as a result the animals become more vulnerable to diseases and defects.

Some observers fear that even the African lion is doomed to decline, destined to become only a tourist attraction in a handful of parks. Others hope that careful management—enforcing laws against poaching, creating protected corridors between parks and sanctuaries, perhaps even importing males from other areas to enrich breeding stock—will allow the African lion to flourish.

In *Prides: The Lions of Moremi* (2000), Pieter Kat, a biologist, wrote,

> *Among the world's predators, there is arguably none that quickens our passion more than the lion. Richly represented in mythology, art, and parable, lions play a major role in the heritage of a diversity of cultures. What are the roots of this attraction to lions? Their sleek beauty and latent power, their grace and serene elegance must play a part, but it is also likely that our fascination stems from an ancestral respect and fear.*

The people of today will determine whether future generations have the chance to experience that ancient respect, fear, and awe.

Glossary

adapt—change or develop in ways that aid survival in the environment

ancestral—having to do with lines of descent or earlier forms

carnivore—animal that eats meat

conservation—action or movement aimed at saving or preserving wildlife or its habitat

diurnal—active during the day

evolve—to change over time; evolution is the process by which new species, or types of plants and animals, emerge from old ones

extinct—no longer existing; died out

felid—member of Felidae, the family that includes all cats

feline—relating to cats

feral—relating to an animal that was once domestic or is descended from domestic animals but that lives as a wild animal

genetic—having to do with genes, the material within the cells of living organisms that transmit characteristics from parents to offspring

habitat—type of environment in which an animal lives

leonine—relating to lions

mammal—animal with a backbone that nourishes its young with milk from its mammary glands. Cats and humans are mammals, as are thousands of other animals

nocturnal—active at night

paleontologist—a scientist who practices paleontology, the study of ancient and extinct life forms, usually by examining fossil remains

predatory—having to do with predation, which is killing for food

prehistoric—before the invention of writing and the beginning of written history

pugmark—the footprint of a big cat

subspecies—variety that forms a distinct population or subgroup within a species

Subspecies Checklist

Scientific name	Common name	Range
Panthera leo leo	Barbary lion	North Africa*
Panthera leo bleyenberghi	Angola lion	Angola, Zimbabwe, Congo
Panthera leo massaicus	Masai lion	Kenya, Tanzania
Panthera leo senegalensis	Senegalese lion	West Africa
Panthera leo krugeri	Transvaal lion	South Africa
Panthera leo melanochaitus	Cape lion	South Africa*
Panthera leo persica	Asiatic lion	Gir Forest, India

*Extinct in the wild.

Further Research

Books for Young People

Arnold, Catherine. *Lion*. New York: Morrow Junior Books, 1995.

Bocknek, Jonathan. *Lions*. Austin, TX: Raintree Steck-Vaughn, 2002.

Clutten-Brock, Juliet. *Cat*. New York: Knopf/Dorling Kindersley, 1991.

Darling, Kathy. *Lions*. Minneapolis, MN: CarolRhoda Books, 2000.

Harman, Amanda. *Lions*. New York: Benchmark Books, 1997.

Jordan, Bill. *Lion*. Austin, TX: Raintree Steck-Vaughn, 2000.

Klevansky, Rhonda. *Big Cats*. London: Lorenz, 1999.

Winner, Cherie and others. *Big Cats*. Minnetonka, MN: NorthWord Press, 2002.

Videos

A Lion's World. Discovery Video, n.d.

Eternal Enemies: Lion and Hyena. National Geographic, 1992.

Lions of the African Night. National Geographic, 1987.

Lions of Darkness. National Geographic, 1997.

Lions: Kings of the Serengeti. Direct Source, 1995.

Web Sites

www.lionresearch.org
> The University of Minnesota's Lion Research Center page maintains links to information about ongoing research projects involving lions, as well as to video clips and articles in magazines such as National Geographic and Science.

www.fmnh.org/exhibits/exhibit_sites/tsavo/default.htm
> The Field Museum of Natural History in Chicago's Web site, Man-Eaters at the Field Museum, focuses on the history and mythology of the lions of Tsavo National Park in Kenya. Includes descriptions of current research.

www.asiatic-lion.org

The Asiatic Lion Information Centre site offers information about the Asiatic lion and current conservation efforts. Includes photos.

www.oakloandzoo.org/atoz/azlion.html

The online animal guide maintained by the Oakland Zoo has an African lion page that features a fact sheet, the sound of a lion's roar, and several video clips.

http://dspace.dial.pipex.com/agarman/lion.htm

The Lion page of the Big Cats Online site consists of a detailed fact sheet.

www.african-lion.org

The African Lion Working Group site concentrates on conservation efforts and offers links to other informative sites.

Bibliography

These books were especially useful to the author in researching this volume.

Adamson, Joy. *Born Free*. New York: Buccaneer Books, 1994.

Bertram, Brian. *Lions*. Stillwater, MN: Voyageur Press, 1998.

Brakefield, Tom. *Big Cats: Kingdom of Might*. Stillwater, MN: Voyageur Press, 1993.
  A thorough and well-illustrated reference work with a general chapter on big-cat evolution, biology, and ecology and a chapter on lions.

Caputo, Philip. *Ghosts of Tsavo: Tracking the Mythic Lions of East Africa*. Washington, DC: National Geographic, 2002.
  A journalist and novelist explores the tangled history of East Africa's famous maneless "man-eaters."

Grace, Eric S. *The Nature of Lions: Social Cats of the Savannas*. Buffalo, NY: Firefly Books, 2001.
  Outstanding photographs by wildlife and nature photographer Art Wolfe.

Joubert, Dereck, and Beverly Joubert. *Hunting with the Moon: The Lions of Savuti*. Washington, DC: National Geographic, 1997.

Kat, Pieter W. *Prides: The Lions of Moremi*. Washington, D.C.: Smithsonian Library Press, 2000.
  A detailed survey of four prides in Botswana's Okavango Delta.

Schaller, George. *The Serengeti Lion*. Chicago: University of Chicago Press, 1972.
  Based on wildlife biologist Schaller's three-year study of lions in East Africa, this book won the 1972 National Book Award and is still considered one of the most informative and important works on lions.

Thomas, Elizabeth Marshall. *The Tribe of Tiger: Cats and Their Culture*. New York: Simon & Schuster, 1994.
  A look at behavior in all species of felines, including lions.

Index

Page numbers in **boldface** are illustrations.

About the Author

REBECCA STEFOFF has written many books on scientific and historical subjects for children and young adults. Among her books on animal life are *Tigers* and *Cats* in Marshall Cavendish's AnimalWays series and the eighteen volumes of the Living Things series, also published by Marshall Cavendish. Stefoff lives in Portland, Oregon. More information about her books for young readers is available at www.rebeccastefoff.com.